LLC & S CORP NUGGETS

What You Need to Know About:
Benefits for Different Business
Entities & Federal and State Tax Rates for
Different Business Entities

MADE SIMPLE

DR. ROSIE MILLIGAN

Published And Distributed By
Professional Publishing House
1425 W. Manchester Ave. Ste B
Los Angeles, California 90047
323-750-3592
Email: professionalpublishinghouse@yahoo.com
www.Professionalpublishinghouse.com

Cover design: TWA Solutions
First printing August 2024
978-1-7328982-8-8
10987654321

Disclaimer:

This book is your essential guide to understanding the many benefits and advantages of choosing the right business entity, as well as providing you the information you need to know about federal and state tax rates for various entities across different states. With this knowledge in hand, you'll be better prepared to select the business entity that best suits your unique needs and circumstances, ensuring a solid foundation for your entrepreneurial journey.

While this book is filled with invaluable information, it is not a substitute for professional legal and tax advice. I strongly encourage you to seek the expertise of a qualified attorney to address any legal concerns regarding your business entity. Additionally, consulting with a certified tax accountant is essential for obtaining tailored tax advice that aligns with your individual circumstances. These professionals will provide you with personalized guidance, ensuring that all legal and tax aspects of your business are handled correctly and efficiently.

Although I am not a certified attorney or tax professional, my decades of firsthand experience as a successful business owner, seasoned senior estate planner, business consultant, and business coach have equipped me with the knowledge and expertise to guide you effectively. Having led numerous thriving ventures and assisted countless individuals in navigating the complexities of entrepreneurship, I have amassed a wealth of practical insights that I am eager to share with you.

TABLE OF CONTENTS

Preface

Acknowledgments, Dedications, and Thanks

About the Author

Chapter 1 Tax Benefits for the Sole Proprietor

Chapter 2 Tax Benefits for a Limited Partnership

Chapter 3 Tax Benefits for an S Corp

Chapter 4 Tax Benefits for a C Corp

Chapter 5 Tax Benefits for a single-member LLC.

Chapter 6 Tax Benefits for a multi-member LLC

Chapter 7 Personal Income Tax Rate

Chapter 8 Federal Income Tax Rate for an S Corp

Chapter 9 Federal Income Tax Rate for a C Corporation

Chapter 10 Federal Income Tax for a single-member LLC

Chapter 11 Federal Income Tax for Multi-member LLC

Chapter 12 Federal Income Tax for a Limited Partnership

Chapter 13 Federal Income Tax for a General Partnership

Chapter 14 State Tax for an LLC

Chapter 15 State Tax for an Individual

Chapter 16 State Tax for an S Corporation

Chapter 17 State Tax for a C Corporation

Chapter 18 State Tax for a Limited Partnership

Chapter 19 State Tax for a General Partnership

ACKNOWLEDGMENTS, DEDICATIONS, AND THANKS
From Dr. Rosie Milligan

First and foremost, I want to thank my late father, Simon Hunter, a Mississippi farmer whose legacy extends far beyond his work in the fields. As an entrepreneur who owned his farm, he introduced me to the world of business at the age of thirteen. I vividly remember selling watermelons from his patch, learning the basics of "Marketing 101." When I asked my father, "How do you know how much to plant each year?" He replied, "I know how much my children will eat, and I know how much the neighbors will steal." This wisdom has shaped my business expectations—always striving to get the most out of every opportunity.

I also want to express my deepest gratitude to my dear sister and best friend, Attorney Clara King. Her insights into the legal aspects of business have been invaluable, and she trained me to become one of Los Angeles's top estate planners.

This book is dedicated to every entrepreneur, regardless of the level of success you have achieved. Your determination to carve out your own path is commendable, and I applaud your courage and perseverance.

I dedicate this book to my youngest son and business sidekick, Cedric Andrea Milligan, Sr. Your unwavering support during our travels and dedication to maintaining the business in my absence is invaluable. Your inspiration ignited my passion for educating aspiring entrepreneurs about the benefits of choosing the LLC business entity. Thank you for being my rock and driving force on this incredible journey.

A heartfelt thank you to my children: Pamela Milligan-McGee, M.D., John Sherman Milligan, Jr., and Cedric Andrea Milligan, Sr. Your unwavering encouragement and support has been invaluable. Your cooperation allowed me to travel the country for lectures and book signings with peace of mind, knowing you were taking care of everything at home. This book is as much a testament to your support as it is to my efforts.

ABOUT DR. ROSIE MILLIGAN

Dr. Rosie Milligan, a woman who knows no limits, is a prominent figure in the business and financial world, known for her multifaceted roles and exceptional expertise. As the CEO of Professional Business Management & Consulting Services and the Founder of My Tech Academy, she has established herself as one of Los Angeles's renowned financial gurus. Her extensive background includes being a seasoned senior estate planner, business coach, business consultant, and holder of a Ph.D. in Business Administration. Her motto: "Erase 'NO,' Step Over 'CAN'T,' and Move Forward With Life" has been a motivating influence for hundreds to whom she has been a mentor and role model.

Dr. Milligan's reputation extends nationwide, with individuals and organizations seeking her out for top-tier business and financial coaching services. With over twenty-six authored books and four hundred fifty books published for other authors, she owns the largest and most prominent African American publishing house in the nation. In addition, she hosts a weekly talk show that further solidifies her influence and reach.

Dr. Milligan's approach revolves around imparting expert guidance to bid farewell to mediocrity. Leveraging her impressive educational achievements, a wealth of business experiences, and years spent consulting non-profit organizations, startups, and established businesses, she offers membership packages that incorporate her personalized coaching methods and proven, effective business strategies. This combination has consistently produced tangible results, ensuring a pathway to a thriving business.

Want to learn more about Dr. Rosie?
Visit her websites:
https://drrosie.com/ or mytechacademy.net.

PREFACE

Starting a business is more than just a way to generate wealth; it's a path to creating a lasting legacy and generational wealth for your family. In today's rapidly evolving world, it is more critical than ever to failproof your business. There was a time when, if frustrated with their business, individuals could confidently say, "Forget it, I am going back to my corporate job." However, the landscape has changed, and corporate jobs are no longer as plentiful.

Technological advancements and AI (Artificial Intelligence) have drastically reduced the number of employees needed in many industries, pushing many to start businesses by default. Unfortunately, many of these new entrepreneurs lack prior business education or work experience.

It is crucial for aspiring business owners to gather as much information as possible about the business entity they choose. Understanding the benefits, advantages, and disadvantages of different business entities can save you time and money and increase your chances of success.

Americans are acutely aware of losses, having faced significant personal and business setbacks due to fires, storms, tornadoes, floods, riots, and the COVID-19 pandemic. Consequently, many people are exploring every option to protect their personal assets for themselves and future generations. As a result, LLCs and S Corporations have become the preferred entities for small business owners.

Empowering yourself with proper business knowledge and understanding of Federal and State Tax regulations will enhance your chances of business success. Remember, the more you learn, the more you can earn. Be a sponge and continuously absorb knowledge. Knowledge is to success as water is to plants.

I look forward to seeing you at the top.

CHAPTER 1

Tax Benefits for the Sole Proprietor

As a sole proprietor, there are several tax benefits and advantages you can enjoy. Here are the key tax benefits for a sole proprietorship:

Pass-Through Taxation:
- **Avoidance of Double Taxation**: A sole proprietorship is not taxed as a separate entity. Instead, the business's income, deductions, and credits pass through to the owner's personal tax return. This avoids the double taxation faced by C Corporations, where income is taxed at both the corporate and shareholder levels.

Simplified Tax Filing:
- **Schedule C**: Sole proprietors report their business income and expenses on Schedule C (Form 1040)

of their personal tax return. This simplifies the tax filing process, as there is no need to file a separate corporate tax return.

Business Expense Deductions:
- **Deductible Expenses**: Sole proprietors can deduct ordinary and necessary business expenses on their personal tax return. This includes expenses such as office supplies, rent, utilities, travel, advertising, and equipment.

Home Office Deduction:
- **Home Office**: If the sole proprietor uses part of their home exclusively for business purposes, they may be eligible for a home office deduction. This can include a portion of mortgage interest, property taxes, utilities, and home maintenance.

Self-Employment Tax:
- **Deductions for Self-Employment Tax**: While sole proprietors are subject to self-employment taxes (Social Security and Medicare) on their net earnings, they can deduct the employer-equivalent portion of self-employment tax (50%) on their personal tax return.

Qualified Business Income (QBI) Deduction:

- **QBI Deduction**: Under the Tax Cuts and Jobs Act of 2017, sole proprietors may be eligible for the Qualified Business Income (QBI) deduction, which allows for a deduction of up to 20% of qualified business income, subject to certain limitations and thresholds.

Flexibility in Accounting:

- **Cash or Accrual Basis**: Sole proprietors can choose to use either the cash or accrual method of accounting, providing flexibility in how income and expenses are reported.

Capital Gains Treatment:

- **Capital Gains**: Income generated from the sale of business assets that are considered capital assets may be taxed at lower long-term capital gains rates if the assets have been held for more than one year.

Retirement Plan Contributions:

- **Retirement Plans**: Sole proprietors can establish and contribute to various retirement plans, such as a Solo 401(k), SEP IRA, or SIMPLE IRA. Contributions to these plans can be tax-deductible, reducing taxable income and helping to save for retirement.

Health Insurance Deduction:

- **Health Insurance**: Sole proprietors can deduct health insurance premiums for themselves, their spouse, and their dependents. This deduction is taken directly on their personal tax return and can help lower taxable income.

Flexibility in Business Structure:

- **Easy Formation and Operation**: Sole proprietorships are the simplest and least expensive business structure to form and operate, with fewer regulatory requirements and administrative costs.

State and Local Tax Considerations:

- **Potential State Benefits**: Depending on the state, there may be additional tax benefits or incentives for operating as a sole proprietor. Some states may offer lower tax rates or exemptions from certain state-level taxes.

Charitable Contributions:

- **Deductible Donations**: Charitable contributions made personally by the sole proprietor can be deducted on their personal tax return, which can reduce taxable income.

While these benefits are advantageous, it's important to be aware of the potential drawbacks of a sole proprietorship, such as unlimited personal liability for business debts and obligations. Consulting with a tax professional or legal advisor can help ensure that you fully understand the implications and optimize your tax situation.

CHAPTER 2

Tax Benefits for a Limited Partnership

A Limited Partnership (LP) offers several tax benefits that can make it an attractive business structure. Here are some key tax advantages:

Pass-Through Taxation:
- **Avoidance of Double Taxation**: Like S Corporations and LLCs, Limited Partnerships enjoy pass-through taxation. This means the partnership itself is not subject to federal income taxes. Instead, the profits and losses are passed through to individual partners, who report them on their personal tax returns. This avoids the double taxation that C Corporations face, where income is taxed at both the corporate and shareholder levels.

Flexibility in Income Allocation:

- **Deductibility of Losses: Special Allocations**: Limited Partnerships can allocate income, gains, losses, deductions, and credits among partners in ways that do not necessarily reflect their ownership percentages. This allows for more flexible financial planning and can optimize the tax situation for each partner.

- **Losses Passed Through**: Losses incurred by the partnership can be passed through to the partners, who can then use these losses to offset other income on their personal tax returns, subject to certain limitations such as the at-risk and passive activity loss rules.

Self-Employment Taxes:

- **Capital Gains Treatment: Limited Partners**: Limited partners are generally not considered active participants in the business, which means they do not have to pay self-employment taxes (Social Security and Medicare taxes) on their share of the partnership's income. This can result in significant tax savings.

- **Capital Gains**: Income generated from the sale of partnership assets that are considered capital assets may be taxed at the lower long-term capital gains rates if the assets have been held for more than a year.

Estate Planning:

- **Valuation Discounts**: For estate planning purposes, interests in a Limited Partnership can sometimes be valued at a discount due to lack of control and marketability, potentially reducing the taxable value of the estate.

Qualified Business Income Deduction:

- **QBI Deduction**: Under the Tax Cuts and Jobs Act of 2017, partners in a Limited Partnership may be eligible for the Qualified Business Income (QBI) deduction, which allows for a deduction of up to 20% of qualified business income from a pass-through entity, subject to certain limitations and thresholds.

State and Local Tax Considerations:

- **State-Level Benefits**: Some states may offer additional tax benefits or incentives for forming a Limited Partnership, such as lower state income tax rates or exemptions from certain state-level taxes.

Flexibility in Contributions and Distributions:
- **Flexibility**: Limited Partnerships offer flexibility in how partners can contribute to and withdraw from the business. Contributions can be made in cash, property, or services, and distributions can be structured in a tax-efficient manner.

While Limited Partnerships offer these benefits, it's important to note that limited partners have no say in the day to day operation of the business. Consulting with a tax professional or legal advisor is advisable to fully understand the implications and to structure the partnership in the most beneficial way.

CHAPTER 3

Tax Benefits for an S Corp

An S Corporation (S Corp) offers several tax benefits that can be advantageous for small business owners. Here are the key tax benefits:

Pass-Through Taxation:
- **Avoidance of Double Taxation**: Like Limited Partnerships and LLCs, S Corps enjoy pass-through taxation. This means the corporation itself is not subject to federal income taxes. Instead, income, deductions, credits, and other tax items pass through to shareholders, who report them on their personal tax returns. This avoids the double taxation faced by C Corporations.

Reduced Self-Employment Taxes:
- **Salary and Dividends**: Shareholders of an S Corp, who are also employees, can receive a reasonable

salary, which is subject to payroll taxes (Social Security and Medicare). However, the remaining profits can be distributed as dividends, which are not subject to self-employment taxes. This can result in significant tax savings.

Tax Deductions:

- **Business Expense Deductions**: S Corps can deduct ordinary and necessary business expenses before distributing income to shareholders. This includes salaries, rent, utilities, travel expenses, and more.

- **Qualified Business Income (QBI) Deduction**: Under the Tax Cuts and Jobs Act of 2017, shareholders of an S Corp may be eligible for the QBI deduction, which allows for a deduction of up to 20% of qualified business income, subject to certain limitations and thresholds.

Flexibility in Accounting:

- **Cash Method of Accounting**: S Corps are generally allowed to use the cash method of accounting if they meet certain criteria, which can simplify record-keeping and defer income recognition.

Fringe Benefits:

- **Employee Benefits**: Shareholders who are also employees can receive certain fringe benefits, such as health insurance and retirement plan contributions, which may be deductible by the S Corp and not taxable to the employee shareholders.

Limited Liability Protection:

- **Limited Liability**: While not a direct tax benefit, the limited liability protection provided to S Corp shareholders can indirectly protect personal assets, potentially reducing financial risks associated with tax liabilities.

Estate Planning:

- **Ownership Transfer**: S Corp shares can be easily transferred to family members, which can be advantageous for estate planning and succession planning, potentially reducing estate tax liabilities.

State and Local Tax Considerations:

- **State-Level Benefits**: Some states may offer additional tax benefits or incentives for forming an S Corp, such as lower state income tax rates or exemptions from certain state-level taxes.

Corporate Losses:
- **Pass-Through of Losses**: Losses incurred by the S Corp can be passed through to shareholders, who can then use these losses to offset other income on their personal tax returns, subject to certain limitations such as the at-risk and passive activity loss rules.

Basis Adjustments:
- **Increase in Basis**: Shareholders can increase their basis in the S Corp by their share of the corporation's income, which can provide tax benefits when they sell their shares or receive distributions.

While S Corps offers these tax benefits, there are also certain restrictions and compliance requirements. For instance, S Corps are limited to 100 shareholders, all of whom must be U.S. citizens or residents, and can only issue one class of stock. It's advisable to consult with a tax professional or legal advisor to fully understand the implications and to determine if an S Corp is the best structure for your business.

CHAPTER 4

Tax Benefits for a C Corp

A C Corporation (C Corp) offers several tax benefits that can be advantageous for businesses, particularly those that plan to grow, raise capital, or reinvest earnings. Here are the key tax benefits of a C Corp:

Flat Corporate Tax Rate:
- **21% Flat Rate**: The Tax Cuts and Jobs Act of 2017 set the federal corporate income tax rate at a flat 21%. This can be beneficial for profitable companies, particularly those that would face higher individual tax rates in a pass-through entity structure.

Deductibility of Business Expenses:
- **Comprehensive Deductions**: C Corps can deduct a wide range of ordinary and necessary business expenses, including salaries, rent, utilities, travel expenses, advertising costs, and employee benefits such as health insurance and retirement plan contributions.

Fringe Benefits:
- **Tax-Free Benefits**: C Corps can provide a variety of fringe benefits to employees (including shareholder-employees) that are deductible by the corporation and not taxable to the employees. These can include health insurance, life insurance, retirement plan contributions, educational assistance, and other employee benefits.

Retained Earnings:
- **Reinvestment**: Unlike pass-through entities, C Corps can retain and reinvest earnings in the business without those earnings being immediately taxed to shareholders. This allows the company to fund growth and expansion projects more efficiently.

No Limit on Shareholders:
- **Unlimited Shareholders**: C Corps can have an unlimited number of shareholders, which makes it easier to raise capital through the sale of stock. Additionally, there are no restrictions on the types of shareholders (e.g., individuals, other corporations, foreign investors).

Multiple Classes of Stock:
- **Flexibility in Ownership Structure**: C Corps can issue multiple classes of stock, each with different rights, preferences, and privileges. This flexibility can be advantageous for structuring investments and attracting different types of investors.

Lower Capital Gains Rates:
- **Qualified Small Business Stock (QSBS)**: If a C Corp qualifies as a Qualified Small Business (QSB) and certain requirements are met, shareholders may be eligible to exclude up to 100% of the gain on the sale of their stock if it has been held for more than five years. The gain exclusion can be a significant tax benefit for investors.

Charitable Contributions:
- **Deductible Donations**: C Corps can deduct charitable contributions up to 10% of their taxable income, providing a benefit for companies that engage in philanthropy.

Net Operating Losses (NOLs):
- **Carryforwards and Carrybacks**: C Corps can use net operating losses to offset taxable income in future years, which can help smooth out tax

liabilities over time. Currently, NOLs can be carried forward indefinitely to offset up to 80% of taxable income in a given year.

State and Local Tax Planning:
- **Potential Benefits**: Depending on the state, there may be additional tax advantages or incentives for operating as a C Corp. Some states may offer lower corporate tax rates or other benefits that can further reduce the overall tax burden.

Tax Deferral on Gains:
- **Section 1202 Exclusion**: As mentioned earlier, under Section 1202 of the Internal Revenue Code, gains from the sale of qualified small business stock held for more than five years can be excluded from federal income tax, subject to specific conditions and limitations.

While these benefits can be substantial, it's important to consider the potential drawbacks of a C Corp, such as the possibility of double taxation (once at the corporate level and again at the shareholder level when dividends are distributed). Consulting with a tax professional or legal advisor is advisable to determine if a C Corp is the best structure for your business based on its specific circumstances and goals.

CHAPTER 5

Tax Benefits for a Single-Member LLC

A single-member LLC offers several tax benefits that can be advantageous for small business owners. Here are the key tax benefits:

Pass-Through Taxation:
- **Avoidance of Double Taxation**: By default, a single-member LLC is treated as a disregarded entity for federal income tax purposes. This means that the LLC itself is not subject to federal income taxes. Instead, the LLC's income, deductions, and credits pass through to the owner, who reports these items on their personal tax return. This avoids the double taxation faced by C Corporations.

Simplified Tax Filing:
- **Schedule C**: The owner of a single-member LLC reports business income and expenses on Schedule C of their personal Form 1040. This simplifies the tax filing process, as there is no need to file a separate corporate tax return.

Business Expense Deductions:
- **Deductible Expenses**: The owner can deduct ordinary and necessary business expenses on their personal tax return. This includes expenses such as office supplies, rent, utilities, travel, and equipment.

Self-Employment Tax:
- **Flexible Tax Planning**: While all net earnings from the business are subject to self-employment taxes (Social Security and Medicare), the owner has the option to elect corporate taxation by filing Form 8832, Entity Classification Election. If the LLC elects to be taxed as an S Corporation, the owner can potentially reduce self-employment tax by taking a reasonable salary and distributing the remaining profits as dividends.

Qualified Business Income Deduction:

- **QBI Deduction**: Under the Tax Cuts and Jobs Act of 2017, the owner of a single-member LLC may be eligible for the Qualified Business Income (QBI) deduction, which allows for a deduction of up to 20% of qualified business income. This can significantly reduce taxable income.

Flexibility in Accounting:

- **Cash or Accrual Basis**: The owner can choose to use either the cash or accrual method of accounting, providing flexibility in how income and expenses are reported.

Limited Liability Protection:

- **Legal Protection**: While not a direct tax benefit, the limited liability protection provided by an LLC can indirectly protect the owner's personal assets from business debts and liabilities, potentially reducing financial risks associated with tax liabilities.

Capital Gains Treatment:

- **Capital Gains**: Income generated from the sale of LLC assets that are considered capital assets may be taxed at the lower long-term capital gains rates if the assets have been held for more than a year.

Estate Planning:
- **Ownership Transfer**: An LLC structure can facilitate the transfer of ownership interests as part of estate planning, potentially reducing estate tax liabilities and simplifying succession planning.

State and Local Tax Considerations:
- **Potential State Benefits**: Depending on the state, there may be additional tax advantages or incentives for operating as a single-member LLC. Some states may offer lower tax rates or exemptions from certain state-level taxes.

Home Office Deduction:
- **Home Office**: If the owner uses part of their home exclusively for business purposes, they may be eligible for a home office deduction, which can include a portion of mortgage interest, property taxes, utilities, and home maintenance.

While these benefits can be substantial, it's important to consider the potential drawbacks and compliance requirements of an SMLLC. Consulting with a tax professional or legal advisor is advisable to fully understand the implications and to ensure the business is structured most beneficially.

CHAPTER 6

Tax Benefits for a Multi-Member LLC

A multi-member LLC offers several tax benefits that can be advantageous for business owners. Here are the key tax benefits:

Pass-Through Taxation:
- **Avoidance of Double Taxation**: By default, a multi-member LLC is treated as a partnership for federal income tax purposes. This means that the LLC itself is not subject to federal income taxes. Instead, the LLC's income, deductions, and credits pass through to members, who report these items on their personal tax returns. This avoids the double taxation faced by C Corporations.

Flexibility in Income Allocation:
- **Special Allocations**: Members can agree to allocate income, gains, losses, deductions, and

credits in ways that do not necessarily reflect their ownership percentages, as long as the allocations have a substantial economic effect. This allows for more flexible financial planning and can optimize the tax situation for each member.

Business Expense Deductions:
- **Deductible Expenses**: The LLC can deduct ordinary and necessary business expenses before distributing income to the members. This includes expenses such as office supplies, rent, utilities, travel, and equipment.

Self-Employment Tax:
- **Flexibility in Taxation**: By default, members of an LLC are subject to self-employment taxes (Social Security and Medicare) on their share of the LLC's income. However, the LLC can elect to be taxed as an S Corporation by filing Form 2553, which may allow members to receive a portion of their income as dividends not subject to self-employment tax.

Qualified Business Income Deduction:
- **QBI Deduction**: Under the Tax Cuts and Jobs Act of 2017, members of a multi-member LLC

may be eligible for the Qualified Business Income (QBI) deduction, which allows for a deduction of up to 20% of qualified business income, subject to certain limitations and thresholds.

Basis Adjustments:

- **Increase in Basis**: Members can increase their basis in the LLC by their share of the LLC's income, which can provide tax benefits when they sell their interests or receive distributions.

Flexibility in Accounting:

- **Cash or Accrual Basis**: The LLC can choose to use either the cash or accrual method of accounting, providing flexibility in how income and expenses are reported.

Limited Liability Protection:

- **Legal Protection**: While not a direct tax benefit, the limited liability protection provided by an LLC can indirectly protect members' personal assets from business debts and liabilities, potentially reducing financial risks associated with tax liabilities.

Capital Gains Treatment:
- **Capital Gains**: Income generated from the sale of LLC assets that are considered capital assets may be taxed at the lower long-term capital gains rates if the assets have been held for more than a year.

Estate Planning:
- **Ownership Transfer**: An LLC structure can facilitate the transfer of ownership interests as part of estate planning, potentially reducing estate tax liabilities and simplifying succession planning.

State and Local Tax Considerations:
- **Potential State Benefits**: Depending on the state, there may be additional tax advantages or incentives for operating as a multi-member LLC. Some states may offer lower tax rates or exemptions from certain state-level taxes.

Home Office Deduction:
- **Home Office**: If any members use part of their homes exclusively for business purposes, they may be eligible for a home office deduction, which can include a portion of mortgage interest, property taxes, utilities, and home maintenance.

Employee Benefits:
- **Fringe Benefits:** The LLC can provide a variety of fringe benefits to employees (including member-employees) that are deductible by the LLC and not taxable to the employees. These can include health insurance, retirement plan contributions, and other employee benefits.

Charitable Contributions:
- **Deductible Donations:** The LLC can make charitable contributions and deduct them as business expenses, providing a benefit for companies that engage in philanthropy.

While these benefits can be substantial, it's important to consider the potential complexities and compliance requirements of a multi-member LLC. To fully understand the implications and ensure the business is structured most beneficially, it is advisable to consult with a tax professional or legal advisor.

CHAPTER 7

Personal Income Tax Rate

For Single Filers:
- **10%** on income up to $11,000
- **12%** on income over $11,000 up to $44,725
- **22%** on income over $44,725 up to $95,375
- **24%** on income over $95,375 up to $182,100
- **32%** on income over $182,100 up to $231,250
- **35%** on income over $231,250 up to $578,125
- **37%** on income over $578,125

For Married Individuals Filing Jointly:
- **10%** on income up to $22,000
- **12%** on income over $22,000 up to $89,450
- **22%** on income over $89,450 up to $190,750
- **24%** on income over $190,750 up to $364,200
- **32%** on income over $364,200 up to $462,500
- **35%** on income over $462,500 up to $693,750
- **37%** on income over $693,750

For Heads of Household:
- **10%** on income up to $15,700

- **12%** on income over $15,700 up to $59,850
- **22%** on income over $59,850 up to $95,350
- **24%** on income over $95,350 up to $182,100
- **32%** on income over $182,100 up to $231,250
- **35%** on income over $231,250 up to $578,100
- **37%** on income over $578,100

For Married Individuals Filing Separately:
- **10%** on income up to $11,000
- **12%** on income over $11,000 up to $44,725
- **22%** on income over $44,725 up to $95,375
- **24%** on income over $95,375 up to $182,100
- **32%** on income over $182,100 up to $231,250
- **35%** on income over $231,250 up to $346,875
- **37%** on income over $346,875

CHAPTER 8

Federal Income Tax Rate for an S Corp

A n S Corporation (S Corp) itself is generally not subject to federal income tax at the corporate level. Instead, its income, deductions, credits, and other tax items pass through to its shareholders, who then report these items on their individual income tax returns. Therefore, the tax rate for an S Corp's income depends on the individual federal income tax rates of the shareholders.

Federal Individual Income Tax Rates for 2024:

For Single Filers:
- 10% on income up to $11,000
- 12% on income over $11,000 up to $44,725
- 22% on income over $44,725 up to $95,375
- 24% on income over $95,375 up to $182,100
- 32% on income over $182,100 up to $231,250

- 35% on income over $231,250 up to $578,125
- 37% on income over $578,125

For Married Individuals Filing Jointly:
- 10% on income up to $22,000
- 12% on income over $22,000 up to $89,450
- 22% on income over $89,450 up to $190,750
- 24% on income over $190,750 up to $364,200
- 32% on income over $364,200 up to $462,500
- 35% on income over $462,500 up to $693,750
- 37% on income over $693,750

For Heads of Household:
- 10% on income up to $15,700
- 12% on income over $15,700 up to $59,850
- 22% on income over $59,850 up to $95,350
- 24% on income over $95,350 up to $182,100
- 32% on income over $182,100 up to $231,250
- 35% on income over $231,250 up to $578,100
- 37% on income over $578,100

For Married Individuals Filing Separately:
- 10% on income up to $11,000
- 12% on income over $11,000 up to $44,725
- 22% on income over $44,725 up to $95,375
- 24% on income over $95,375 up to $182,100

- 32% on income over $182,100 up to $231,250
- 35% on income over $231,250 up to $346,875
- 37% on income over $346,875

Exceptions Where S Corps Might Be Subject to Tax:

While S Corps rarely pay federal income taxes, there are exceptions where they might be subject to specific federal taxes:

1. **Built-in Gains Tax:** If a corporation that was previously a C Corporation elects to become an S Corporation, it may be subject to a built-in gains tax on appreciated assets held at the time of the conversion if the corporation sells those assets within five years of the conversion.

2. **Excess Net Passive Income Tax:** An S Corp with accumulated earnings and profits from when it was a C Corporation and more than 25% of its gross receipts derived from passive income (e.g., interest, dividends, rents, royalties) might be subject to a tax on its excess net passive income.

3. **LIFO Recapture Tax:** If an S Corp uses the last-in, first-out (LIFO) inventory method, it may be subject to an LIFO recapture tax when it elects S Corporation status.

CHAPTER 9

Federal Income Tax Rate for C Corporations

As of 2024, the federal corporate income tax rate for C Corporations in the United States is a flat **21%**. This rate applies to the corporation's taxable income, regardless of the amount.

In addition to the federal corporate tax rate, C Corporations may also be subject to state and local corporate taxes, which vary by jurisdiction. State corporate tax rates can range from 0% to over 10%, depending on the state. Some cities also impose additional local corporate taxes.

For accurate tax planning and compliance, it's advisable for C Corporations to consult with a tax professional or refer to the specific state and local tax authorities for detailed information.

Federal Income Tax Rate for a Sole Proprietor

For a sole proprietor, the tax rates are based on the individual's personal income tax rates and the self-employment tax rates. Here's a breakdown of how taxes are assessed:

For Single Filers:

- **10%** on income up to $11,000
- **12%** on income over $11,000 up to $44,725
- **22%** on income over $44,725 up to $95,375
- **24%** on income over $95,375 up to $182,100
- **32%** on income over $182,100 up to $231,250
- **35%** on income over $231,250 up to $578,125
- **37%** on income over $578,125

For Married Individuals Filing Jointly:

- **10%** on income up to $22,000
- **12%** on income over $22,000 up to $89,450
- **22%** on income over $89,450 up to $190,750
- **24%** on income over $190,750 up to $364,200
- **32%** on income over $364,200 up to $462,500
- **35%** on income over $462,500 up to $693,750
- **37%** on income over $693,750

For Heads of Household:

- **10%** on income up to $15,700

- **12%** on income over $15,700 up to $59,850
- **22%** on income over $59,850 up to $95,350
- **24%** on income over $95,350 up to $182,100
- **32%** on income over $182,100 up to $231,250
- **35%** on income over $231,250 up to $578,100
- **37%** on income over $578,100

For Married Individuals Filing Separately:
- **10%** on income up to $11,000
- **12%** on income over $11,000 up to $44,725
- **22%** on income over $44,725 up to $95,375
- **24%** on income over $95,375 up to $182,100
- **32%** on income over $182,100 up to $231,250
- **35%** on income over $231,250 up to $346,875
- **37%** on income over $346,875

Self-Employment Tax

Sole proprietors must also pay self-employment taxes on their net earnings, which cover Social Security and Medicare taxes:

- **Social Security Tax**: 12.4% on the first $160,200 of net earnings (for 2024; this limit may change annually).

- **Medicare Tax**: 2.9% of all net earnings.

- **Additional Medicare Tax**: An additional 0.9% Medicare tax applies to earnings over $200,000 for single filers and $250,000 for married couples filing jointly.

Total Self-Employment Tax

Total self-employment tax is 15.3% on net earnings up to the Social Security wage base, plus 2.9% on earnings exceeding that base, with the additional 0.9% Medicare tax applicable for higher income levels.

Self-Employment Tax Deduction

Sole proprietors can deduct the employer-equivalent portion of self-employment tax (50%) on their personal tax return. This deduction is used to reduce their taxable income, although it does not affect net earnings subject to self-employment tax.

Overall Tax Impact

The overall tax rate for a sole proprietor combines their personal income tax rate with their self-employment taxes. Effective tax planning, including potential deductions and credits, can help manage the total tax liability.

CHAPTER 10

Federal Income Tax Rate for a Single-Member LLC

For a single-member LLC, the tax treatment is similar to that of a sole proprietorship for federal income tax purposes. Here's how the tax rates apply:

Federal Income Tax Rates (2024)

Because the IRS typically treats a single-member LLC as a disregarded entity, the income from the LLC passes through to the owner's personal tax return. The owner pays tax on the LLC's income at the individual income tax rates. Here are the federal income tax rates for 2024:

For Single Filers:
- **10%** on income up to $11,000
- **12%** on income over $11,000 up to $44,725

- **22%** on income over $44,725 up to $95,375
- **24%** on income over $95,375 up to $182,100
- **32%** on income over $182,100 up to $231,250
- **35%** on income over $231,250 up to $578,125
- **37%** on income over $578,125

For Heads of Household:
- **10%** on income up to $15,700
- **12%** on income over $15,700 up to $59,850
- **22%** on income over $59,850 up to $95,350
- **24%** on income over $95,350 up to $182,100
- **32%** on income over $182,100 up to $231,250
- **35%** on income over $231,250 up to $578,100
- **37%** on income over $578,100

For Married Individuals Filing Jointly:
- **10%** on income up to $22,000
- **12%** on income over $22,000 up to $89,450
- **22%** on income over $89,450 up to $190,750
- **24%** on income over $190,750 up to $364,200
- **32%** on income over $364,200 up to $462,500
- **35%** on income over $462,500 up to $693,750
- **37%** on income over $693,750

For Married Individuals Filing Separately:
- **10%** on income up to $11,000

- **12%** on income over $11,000 up to $44,725
- **22%** on income over $44,725 up to $95,375
- **24%** on income over $95,375 up to $182,100
- **32%** on income over $182,100 up to $231,250
- **35%** on income over $231,250 up to $346,875
- **37%** on income over $346,875

Self-Employment Tax

As a single-member LLC, the owner is subject to self-employment taxes on the LLC's net earnings, which include:

- **Social Security Tax**: 12.4% on the first $160,200 of net earnings (for 2024; this limit may change annually).

- **Medicare Tax**: 2.9% of all net earnings.

- **Additional Medicare Tax**: An additional 0.9% Medicare tax applies to earnings over $200,000 for single filers and $250,000 for married couples filing jointly.

Total Self-Employment Tax: 15.3% on net earnings up to the Social Security wage base, plus 2.9% on earnings exceeding that base, with the additional 0.9% Medicare tax applicable for higher income levels.

Self-Employment Tax Deduction
Sole proprietors and single-member LLC owners can deduct the employer-equivalent portion of self-employment tax (50%) on their personal tax return. This deduction reduces taxable income but does not affect net earnings subject to self-employment tax.

Election to be Taxed as an S Corporation
If beneficial, the owner of a single-member LLC can elect to have the LLC taxed as an S Corporation by filing Form 2553 with the IRS. This election can allow the owner to take a reasonable salary and distribute additional profits as dividends, potentially reducing self-employment tax liability.

Overall Tax Impact
The total tax liability for a single-member LLC owner combines personal income tax rate with self-employment taxes. Effective tax planning and potential deductions can help manage this liability.

CHAPTER 11

The Federal Income Tax Rate for a Multi-Member LLC

For a multi-member LLC (MMLLC), the tax treatment is similar to that of a partnership for federal income tax purposes. Here's how the tax rates apply:

Federal Income Tax Rates
Pass-Through Taxation:

- **Partnership Taxation**: By default, the IRS treats a multi-member LLC as a partnership for federal tax purposes. The LLC itself does not pay federal income taxes. Instead, the LLC's income, deductions, and credits pass through to individual members, who report these items on their personal tax returns.

- **Individual Tax Rates**: Each member pays tax on their share of the LLC's income at their individual income tax rates. The federal income tax rates for 2024 are:

For Single Filers:
  - **10%** on income up to $11,000
  - **12%** on income over $11,000 up to $44,725
  - **22%** on income over $44,725 up to $95,375
  - **24%** on income over $95,375 up to $182,100
  - **32%** on income over $182,100 up to $231,250
  - **35%** on income over $231,250 up to $578,125
  - **37%** on income over $578,125

For Heads of Household:
  - **10%** on income up to $15,700
  - **12%** on income over $15,700 up to $59,850
  - **22%** on income over $59,850 up to $95,350
  - **24%** on income over $95,350 up to

$182,100

- o **32%** on income over $182,100 up to $231,250
- o **35%** on income over $231,250 up to $578,100
- o **37%** on income over $578,100

For Married Individuals Filing Jointly:

- o **10%** on income up to $22,000
- o **12%** on income over $22,000 up to $89,450
- o **22%** on income over $89,450 up to $190,750
- o **24%** on income over $190,750 up to $364,200
- o **32%** on income over $364,200 up to $462,500
- o **35%** on income over $462,500 up to $693,750
- o **37%** on income over $693,750

For Married Individuals Filing Separately:

- o **10%** on income up to $11,000
- o **12%** on income over $11,000 up to $44,725

- o **22%** on income over $44,725 up to $95,375
- o **24%** on income over $95,375 up to $182,100
- o **32%** on income over $182,100 up to $231,250
- o **35%** on income over $231,250 up to $346,875
- o **37%** on income over $346,875

Self-Employment Tax

Members of a multi-member LLC are subject to self-employment taxes on their share of the LLC's net earnings:

- **Social Security Tax**: 12.4% on the first $160,200 of net earnings (for 2024; this limit may change annually).

- **Medicare Tax**: 2.9% of all net earnings.

- **Additional Medicare Tax**: An additional 0.9% Medicare tax applies to earnings over $200,000 for single filers and $250,000 for married couples filing jointly.

Total Self-Employment Tax

Total self-employment tax is 15.3% on net earnings up to the Social Security wage base, plus 2.9% on earnings exceeding that base, with the additional 0.9% Medicare tax applicable for higher income levels.

Self-Employment Tax Deduction

Members can deduct the employer-equivalent portion of self-employment tax (50%) on their personal tax return. This deduction reduces taxable income but does not affect net earnings subject to self-employment tax.

Election to be Taxed as an S Corporation

A multi-member LLC can elect to be taxed as an S Corporation by filing Form 2553 with the IRS. This election could allow members to take a reasonable salary and distribute additional profits as dividends, potentially reducing self-employment tax liability.

Overall Tax Impact

The total tax liability for a member of a multi-member LLC combines their personal income tax rate with self-employment taxes. Effective tax planning, including deductions and credits, can help manage this liability.

CHAPTER 12

Federal Income Tax for a Limited Partnership

For a Limited Partnership, tax treatment and rates depend on how income is reported and taxed at the individual partner level. Here's a detailed look at the tax rates and treatment for a Limited Partnership:

Federal Income Tax Rates
Pass-Through Taxation:

- **Partnership Taxation**: By default, the IRS treats a Limited Partnership as a partnership for federal tax purposes. The LP itself does not pay federal income taxes. Instead, the LP's income, deductions, and credits pass through to individual partners, who report these items on their personal tax returns.

- **Individual Tax Rates**: Partners pay tax on their share of the LP's income at their individual

47

income tax rates. The federal income tax rates for 2024 are:

For Single Filers:
- **10%** on income up to $11,000
- **12%** on income over $11,000 up to $44,725
- **22%** on income over $44,725 up to $95,375
- **24%** on income over $95,375 up to $182,100
- **32%** on income over $182,100 up to $231,250
- **35%** on income over $231,250 up to $578,125
- **37%** on income over $578,125

For Heads of Household:
- **10%** on income up to $15,700
- **12%** on income over $15,700 up to $59,850
- **22%** on income over $59,850 up to $95,350
- **24%** on income over $95,350 up to $182,100
- **32%** on income over $182,100 up to $231,250

- o **35%** on income over $231,250 up to $578,100
- o **37%** on income over $578,100

For Married Individuals Filing Jointly:
- o **10%** on income up to $22,000
- o **12%** on income over $22,000 up to $89,450
- o **22%** on income over $89,450 up to $190,750
- o **24%** on income over $190,750 up to $364,200
- o **32%** on income over $364,200 up to $462,500
- o **35%** on income over $462,500 up to $693,750
- o **37%** on income over $693,750

For Married Individuals Filing Separately:
- o **10%** on income up to $11,000
- o **12%** on income over $11,000 up to $44,725
- o **22%** on income over $44,725 up to $95,375
- o **24%** on income over $95,375 up to $182,100

- o **32%** on income over $182,100 up to $231,250
- o **35%** on income over $231,250 up to $346,875
- o **37%** on income over $346,875

Self-Employment Tax
General Partners:

- **Self-Employment Tax**: General partners in a Limited Partnership are considered self-employed and are subject to self-employment tax on their share of the LP's income.
  - o **Social Security Tax**: 12.4% on the first $160,200 of net earnings (for 2024; this limit may change annually).
  - o **Medicare Tax**: 2.9% of all net earnings.
  - o **Additional Medicare Tax**: An additional 0.9% Medicare tax applies to earnings over $200,000 for single filers and $250,000 for married couples filing jointly.

Total Self-Employment Tax: 15.3% on net earnings up to the Social Security wage base, plus 2.9% on earnings exceeding that base, with the additional 0.9% Medicare tax applicable for higher income levels.

Limited Partners:
- **Not Subject to Self-Employment Tax**: Limited partners typically do not pay self-employment tax on their share of the LP's income, provided they do not have an active role in managing the partnership. Their income is generally subject to regular income tax.

Self-Employment Tax Deduction
- **Deduction for Self-Employment Tax**: General partners can deduct the employer-equivalent portion of self-employment tax (50%) on their personal tax return. This deduction reduces taxable income but does not affect net earnings subject to self-employment tax.

Election to be Taxed as an S Corporation
- **S Corporation Election**: A Limited Partnership cannot elect to be taxed as an S Corporation, but if the LP has partners that are corporations or other entities, it might affect how the income is reported and taxed. The LP generally remains a partnership for tax purposes unless it is converted into a different entity type.

Overall Tax Impact

The total tax liability for partners in a Limited Partnership combines their personal income tax rate with self-employment taxes (for general partners). Effective tax planning and potential deductions can help manage this liability.

For accurate tax planning and compliance, consulting with a tax professional is advisable to ensure the LP's structure and tax situation are optimized according to current regulations and partners' financial goals.

CHAPTER 13

Federal Tax for a General Partnership

For a general partnership, the tax treatment and rates are similar to those for a Limited Partnership in terms of pass-through taxation. Here's a detailed look at the tax rates and treatment for a general partnership:

Federal Income Tax Rates
Pass-Through Taxation:

- **Partnership Taxation**: A general partnership itself does not pay federal income tax. Instead, the partnership's income, deductions, and credits pass through to individual partners, who report these items on their personal tax returns.

- **Individual Tax Rates**: Partners pay tax on their share of the partnership's income at their individual income tax rates. The federal income tax rates for 2024 are:

For Single Filers:

- **10%** on income up to $11,000
- **12%** on income over $11,000 up to $44,725
- **22%** on income over $44,725 up to $95,375
- **24%** on income over $95,375 up to $182,100
- **32%** on income over $182,100 up to $231,250
- **35%** on income over $231,250 up to $578,125
- **37%** on income over $578,125

For Heads of Household:

- **10%** on income up to $15,700
- **12%** on income over $15,700 up to $59,850
- **22%** on income over $59,850 up to $95,350
- **24%** on income over $95,350 up to $182,100
- **32%** on income over $182,100 up to $231,250
- **35%** on income over $231,250 up to $578,100
- **37%** on income over $578,100

For Married Individuals Filing Jointly:

- **10%** on income up to $22,000
- **12%** on income over $22,000 up to $89,450
- **22%** on income over $89,450 up to $190,750
- **24%** on income over $190,750 up to $364,200
- **32%** on income over $364,200 up to $462,500
- **35%** on income over $462,500 up to $693,750
- **37%** on income over $693,750

For Married Individuals Filing Separately:

- **10%** on income up to $11,000
- **12%** on income over $11,000 up to $44,725
- **22%** on income over $44,725 up to $95,375
- **24%** on income over $95,375 up to $182,100
- **32%** on income over $182,100 up to $231,250
- **35%** on income over $231,250 up to $346,875
- **37%** on income over $346,875

Self-Employment Tax
General Partners:

- **Self-Employment Tax:** General partners are considered self-employed and are subject to self-employment taxes on their share of the partnership's net earnings.
    - **Social Security Tax:** 12.4% on the first $160,200 of net earnings (for 2024; this limit may change annually).

    - **Medicare Tax:** 2.9% of all net earnings.

    - **Additional Medicare Tax:** An additional 0.9% Medicare tax applies to earnings over $200,000 for single filers and $250,000 for married couples filing jointly.

    Total Self-Employment Tax: 15.3% on net earnings up to the Social Security wage base, plus 2.9% on earnings exceeding that base, with the additional 0.9% Medicare tax applicable for higher income levels.

Limited Partners:

- **Not Subject to Self-Employment Tax:** Limited partners generally do not pay self-employment tax on their share of the partnership's income, provided they do not have an active role in managing the partnership. Their income is generally subject to regular income tax.

Self-Employment Tax Deduction

- **Deduction for Self-Employment Tax**: General partners can deduct the employer-equivalent portion of self-employment tax (50%) on their personal tax return. This deduction reduces taxable income but does not affect net earnings subject to self-employment tax.

Overall Tax Impact

The total tax liability for partners in a general partnership combines their personal income tax rate with self-employment taxes (for general partners). Effective tax planning, including potential deductions and credits, can help manage this liability.

In addition to federal taxes, S Corps may also be subject to state and local taxes, which can vary significantly depending on the jurisdiction. Some states impose corporate taxes or fees on different business entities.

For detailed and specific tax planning, it is advisable for C and S Corps and their shareholders to consult with a tax professional or refer to the IRS guidelines and respective state tax authorities.

CHAPTER 14

State Tax Rate for an LLC

The state tax rates for an LLC (Limited Liability Company) can vary significantly depending on the state where the LLC is formed and operates. Generally, an LLC can be taxed as a sole proprietorship, partnership, S corporation, or C corporation, and the state tax treatment can differ accordingly. Here are some key points to consider:

1. **State Income Tax**: Some states impose an income tax on LLCs, which can be based on the net income of the business. The rate varies by state.

2. **Franchise Tax**: Some states require LLCs to pay a franchise tax or an annual fee for the privilege of operating in the state. This can be a flat fee or based on the LLC's income, assets, or other measures.

3. **Gross Receipts Tax**: A few states have a gross receipts tax, which is based on the total revenue of the LLC, regardless of profitability.

4. **Additional Local Taxes**: Some cities and counties may also impose additional taxes or fees on LLCs.

Here are some examples of how different states handle LLC taxation:

- **California**: California imposes an $800 annual minimum franchise tax on LLCs, plus an additional fee based on the LLC's gross income. Additionally, LLCs are subject to the state's income tax.

- **Delaware**: Delaware charges an annual franchise tax and a fee for filing the annual report. The franchise tax for LLCs is a flat fee of $300 per year.

- **Texas**: Texas has a franchise tax, which is essentially a gross receipts tax, called the Texas Margin Tax. The rate depends on the LLC's revenue.

- **Florida**: Florida does not have a franchise tax or an income tax for LLCs that are taxed as partnerships or sole proprietorships. However,

LLCs taxed as corporations are subject to state corporate income tax.

- **Nevada**: Nevada does not have a state income tax, but it has an annual business license fee and a gross receipts tax for businesses with revenue above a certain threshold.

CHAPTER 15

State Tax Rate for an Individual

The state tax rate for an individual varies depending on the state in which the individual resides and earns income. Here are some key points and examples:

States with Progressive Income Tax Rates
These states have tax brackets where the rate increases with income.
- **California:** Rates range from 1% to 13.3% based on income.

- **New York:** Rates range from 4% to 10.9%.

- **New Jersey:** Rates range from 1.4% to 10.75%.

States with Flat Income Tax Rates
These states tax all income at the same rate.
- **Colorado:** 4.4%

- **Illinois**: 4.95%

- **Indiana**: 3.23%

States with No Income Tax

These states do not impose an income tax on individuals.

- **Florida**

- **Texas**

- **Washington**

Additional Considerations

- **Local Income Taxes**: Some states allow cities or counties to levy additional income taxes.

- **Deductions and Credits**: States often have different deductions, exemptions, and credits which can affect the effective tax rate.

- **Alternative Minimum Tax (AMT)**: Some states have an AMT that can affect high-income earners.

Examples
1. **California**:
    - 1% on the first $10,099 of taxable income
    - 2% on income between $10,100 and $23,942

    o Up to 13.3% for income over $1 million

2. **New York:**
    o 4% on income up to $8,500
    o 6.85% on income between $21,400 and $80,650
    o 10.9% on income over $25 million

3. **Texas:**
    o No state income tax

Summary Table of Some States' Tax Rates

State	Tax Rate Range
California	1% - 13.3%
New York	4% - 10.9%
New Jersey	1.4% - 10.75%
Illinois	4.95% (flat rate)
Florida	No state income tax
Texas	No state income tax
Colorado	4.4% (flat rate)

CHAPTER 16

State Tax Rate for an S Corp

The state tax rate for an S Corporation (S Corp) varies depending on the state in which the S Corp is incorporated and operates. S Corps are typically pass-through entities for federal tax purposes, meaning the income is passed through to shareholders, who then report it on their personal tax returns. However, states may treat S Corps differently. Here's an overview of how some states tax S Corps:

States with No Corporate Income Tax

These states do not impose a corporate income tax on S Corps:

- **Nevada**
- **South Dakota**
- **Washington**
- **Wyoming**

States with Franchise or Gross Receipts Taxes

Some states impose a franchise tax or a gross receipts tax on S Corps.

- **California**:
  - Minimum franchise tax of $800 per year.
  - An additional fee based on total income from $0 to $1,000,000 or more.
- **Texas**:
  - Franchise tax (or margin tax) based on the company's revenue. The rate is generally 0.375% for most entities.

States with Corporate Income Taxes

Some states tax the net income of S Corps at the corporate level.

- **New York**:
  - S Corps are subject to a fixed dollar minimum tax, which varies based on New York receipts.
  - For larger S Corps, the tax can range from $25 to $4,500.
- **Illinois**:
  - Personal property replacement tax at a rate of 1.5% of net income.

States with Special S Corp Taxes or Fees
Some states impose special taxes or fees on S Corps.
- **New Jersey**:
  - S Corps must pay an S Corporation Business Tax, which ranges from $375 to $1,500, depending on the amount of New Jersey gross receipts.

Examples of State Tax Treatments for S Corps
1. **California**:
   - Minimum franchise tax: $800.
   - Additional fee based on total income: $0 to $1,000,000 or more.

2. **Texas**:
   - Franchise tax: 0.375% for most entities.

3. **New York**:
   - Fixed dollar minimum tax based on New York receipts: $25 to $4,500.

4. **Illinois**:
   - Personal property replacement tax: 1.5% of net income.

5. **Florida**:
   - No state corporate income tax on S Corps.

6. New Jersey:

- o S Corporation Business Tax: $375 to $1,500 based on gross receipts.

Summary Table of State Tax Treatments for S Corps

State	Tax Type	Rate/Amount
California	Franchise Tax	Minimum $800 + fee based on income
Texas	Franchise Tax	0.375% of revenue
New York	Fixed Dollar Minimum Tax	$25 to $4,500 based on receipts
Illinois	Personal Property Tax	1.5% of net income
Florida	No State Corporate Tax	N/A
New Jersey	S Corporation Business Tax	$375 to $1,500 based on gross receipts

CHAPTER 17

State Tax for a C Corp

The state tax rates for a C Corporation (C Corp) can vary widely depending on the state in which the C Corp is incorporated and operates. Here is an overview of how some states tax C Corps:

States with Corporate Income Taxes

Most states impose a corporate income tax on C Corps, with rates that can be flat or progressive.

1. **California:**

   o Corporate income tax rate: 8.84%.

   o Alternative minimum tax (AMT): 6.65%.

2. **New York:**

   o Corporate income tax rate: 6.5%.

   o Fixed dollar minimum tax based on New York receipts: $25 to $200,000.

3. Texas:

- o No state corporate income tax.

- o Franchise tax (margin tax) based on the company's revenue: 0.375% for retail/ wholesale, 0.75% for other businesses.

4. Florida:

- o Corporate income tax rate: 5.5%.

5. Illinois:

- o Corporate income tax rate: 7% (as of 2020).

- o Additional personal property replacement tax: 2.5%.

States with No Corporate Income Tax

Some states do not impose a corporate income tax on C Corps:

- **Nevada**

- **South Dakota**

- **Washington**

- **Wyoming**

Additional Considerations

- **Franchise Taxes**: Some states impose franchise taxes or other fees in addition to or instead of a corporate income tax.

- **Gross Receipts Taxes**: Some states, like Ohio, impose a commercial activity tax based on gross receipts instead of net income.

- **Local Taxes**: Cities and counties may also impose additional taxes on corporations.

Examples of State Tax Treatments for C Corps

1. **California**:
   o Corporate income tax: 8.84%.
   o AMT: 6.65%.
2. **New York**:
   o Corporate income tax: 6.5%.
   o Fixed dollar minimum tax: $25 to $200,000 based on receipts.
3. **Texas**:
   o No state corporate income tax.
   o Franchise tax: 0.375% for retail/wholesale, 0.75% for other businesses.
4. **Florida**:
   o Corporate income tax: 5.5%.

5. **Illinois:**
   o Corporate income tax: 7%.
   o Personal property replacement tax: 2.5%.

6. **Nevada:**
   o No state corporate income tax.
   o Annual business license fee and a gross receipts tax for businesses with revenue above a certain threshold.

Summary Table of State Tax Rates for C Corps

State	Corporate Income Tax Rate	Additional Taxes/Fees
California	8.84%	6.65% AMT
New York	6.5%	$25 to $200,000 fixed dollar minimum tax based on receipts
Texas	None	Franchise tax: 0.375%/0.75%
Florida	5.5%	None
Illinois	7%	2.5% personal property replacement tax
Nevada	None	Business license fee and gross receipts tax
South Dakota	None	None

State	Corporate Income Tax Rate	Additional Taxes/Fees
Washington	None	Business and occupation (B&O) tax based on gross receipts
Wisconsin	None	

CHAPTER 18

State Tax Rate for a Limited Partnership

The state tax rate for a Limited Partnership (LP) can vary depending on the state in which the LP operates. Limited Partnerships are typically pass-through entities, meaning the income passes through to the partners, who then report it on their personal tax returns. However, some states impose specific taxes or fees on LPs. Here's an overview of how some states handle the taxation of LPs:

States with No Income Tax

Some states do not impose an income tax on individuals or businesses, which can simplify tax obligations for LPs:

- **Alaska**
- **Florida**
- **Nevada**

- **South Dakota**
- **Texas**
- **Washington**
- **Wyoming**

States with Franchise Taxes or Annual Fees

Many states impose franchise taxes or annual fees on LPs:
- **California:**
  - $800 annual minimum franchise tax.
- **Delaware:**
  - Annual franchise tax: $300.
- **Texas:**
  - Franchise tax (margin tax) based on revenue: 0.375% for retail/wholesale and 0.75% for other businesses.

States with Personal Income Tax on Partners

In states with personal income tax, partners must report their share of the LP's income on their personal tax returns. The rates vary by state and can be progressive:
- **New York:**
  - Personal income tax rates range from 4% to 10.9%.
- **California:**
  - Personal income tax rates range from 1% to 13.3%.

Gross Receipts Taxes

Some states impose gross receipts taxes, which are based on the total revenue of the LP:

- **Ohio:**
    - Commercial Activity Tax (CAT): 0.26% on gross receipts over $1 million.

Examples of State Tax Treatments for LPs

1. **California:**
    - $800 annual minimum franchise tax.
    - Partners report income on personal tax returns at rates ranging from 1% to 13.3%.

2. **Texas:**
    - Franchise tax: 0.375% for retail/wholesale and 0.75% for other businesses.
    - No state income tax.

3. **New York:**
    - Partners report income on personal tax returns at rates ranging from 4% to 10.9%.

4. **Florida:**
    - No state income tax or franchise tax.

5. **Ohio:**
    - Commercial Activity Tax: 0.26% on gross receipts over $1 million.

Summary Table of State Tax Treatments for LPs

State	Franchise Tax/ Annual Fee	Personal Income Tax Rate for Partners	Additional Taxes
California	$800 minimum franchise tax	1% - 13.3%	None
Texas	.375%/0.75% franchise tax	None	None
New York	None	4% - 10.9%	None
Florida	None	None	None
Ohio	None	2.765% - 3.99%	0.26% Commercial Activity Tax
Delaware	$300 franchise tax	2.2% - 6.6%	None
Nevada	None	None	None
Washington	None	None	Business and occupation (B&O) tax

CHAPTER 19

State Tax Rate for a General Partnership

General Partnerships are typically pass-through entities, meaning the income is passed through to the partners, who then report it on their personal tax returns. However, some states impose specific taxes or fees on GPs. Here's an overview of how different states handle the taxation of GPs:

States with No Income Tax

Some states do not impose an income tax on individuals or businesses, simplifying tax obligations for GPs:

- **Alaska**

- **Florida**

- **Nevada**

- **South Dakota**

- **Texas**

- **Washington**

- **Wyoming**

States with Franchise Taxes or Annual Fees
Many states impose franchise taxes or annual fees on GPs:
- **California**:
  - $800 annual minimum franchise tax.
- **Delaware**:
  - Annual partnership tax: $300.
- **Texas**:
  - Franchise tax (margin tax) based on revenue: 0.375% for retail/wholesale and 0.75% for other businesses.

States with Personal Income Tax on Partners
In states with personal income tax, partners must report their share of the GP's income on their personal tax returns. The rates vary by state and can be progressive:
- **New York**:
  - Personal income tax rates range from 4% to 10.9%.
- **California**:
  - Personal income tax rates range from 1% to 13.3%.

Gross Receipts Taxes

Some states impose gross receipts taxes, which are based on the total revenue of the GP:

- **Ohio**:
  - ○ Commercial Activity Tax (CAT): 0.26% on gross receipts over $1 million.

Examples of State Tax Treatments for GPs

1. **California**:
   - ○ $800 annual minimum franchise tax.
   - ○ Partners report income on personal tax returns at rates ranging from 1% to 13.3%.

2. **Texas**:
   - ○ Franchise tax: 0.375% for retail/wholesale and 0.75% for other businesses.
   - ○ No state income tax.

3. **New York**:
   - ○ Partners report income on personal tax returns at rates ranging from 4% to 10.9%.

4. **Florida**:
   - ○ No state income tax or franchise tax.

5. **Ohio**:
   - ○ Commercial Activity Tax: 0.26% on gross receipts over $1 million.

Summary Table of State Tax Treatments for GPs

State	Franchise Tax/ Annual Fee	Personal Income Tax Rate for Partners	Additional Taxes
California	$800 minimum franchise tax	1% - 13.3%	None
Texas	0.375%/0.75% franchise tax	None	None
New York	None	4% - 10.9%	None
Florida	None	None	None
Ohio	None	2.765% - 3.99%	0.26% Commercial Activity Tax
Delaware	$300 partnership tax	2.2% - 6.6%	None
Nevada	None	None	None
Washington	None	None	Business and occupation (B&O) tax
Wisconsin	None